"and the skin will be stitched to the tug in the sea
and the stone to the tear in the night
and whatever is made in this way, my love
is all that I can write."

First published 2015 by
Karnac Books Ltd
118 Finchley Road
London NW3 5HT

Copyright © 2015 by Judith Gracie

The right of Judith Gracie to be identified as the author of this work has been asserted in accordance with §§ 77 and 78 of the Copyright Design and Patents Act 1988.

British Library Cataloguing in Publication Data

A C.I.P. for this book is available from the British Library

ISBN-00: 978-1-7822013-8-0

Printed in Great Britain

www.karnacbooks.com

LOST IN SPACE
AME X ANE : PATHS OF IMPOSSIBILITY

LOST IN SPACE
AMEXANE: PATHS OF IMPOSSIBILITY

Judith Gracie

KARNAC

About the Author/s

Judith Gracie has worked in the field of psychoanalysis for many years and is a practising clinician. She lives in London with her three children.

Claire Oerton is her dearest friend and principal interlocutor.

Bernard Burgoyne is a psychologist practising in London. He is a Member of the World Association of Psychoanalysis, and a founder member of the Centre for Freudian Analysis, and is currently Emeritus Professor of Psychoanalysis at Middlesex University. He has published extensively on questions of structure in psychoanalysis, and is particularly concerned with the way in which the predicaments of human interactions are resolvable only by a consideration of the frontiers of desire and the texture of space.

Preface

"The mares which bear me as far as my desires might reach …" – a piece of writing from two and a half thousand years ago catches the intent of this work. The author has etched a body of poetry that follows a trajectory not often encountered in the writings of the modern world. Finding pathways that contest established opinion is itself a research project; making a series of such pathways demands perhaps the voice of a woman. Only a woman, after all, has access to such wider classes of space.

The outline of this work is set out as follows:

Part I   Writing …

Part II   Lost

Part III Tragedy

Part IV   Mother

Part V   Paths

Underlying the disarray of the modern mind there are pathways that at times allow for the finding of a way through: the cost of seeking out these trajectories can be great. Limits to what can be said have been brought into being: a poetic voice challenges such boundaries where they refuse to admit an effectiveness to speech.

Bernard Burgoyne,

London, 2015.

To my little brother ...

Contents

In the beginning . . .

(of which is the offering of this little leaf)

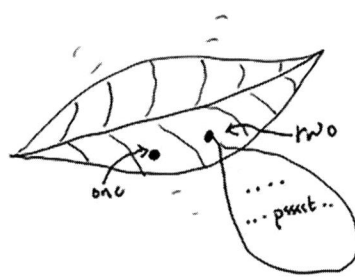

two: ... pssst ...
one: ... s'up, meine kleine? ...
two: ... do you know what it is that in actual fact we are doing ... ? ... actually ...
one: ... hmmm ... I guess, ma petite feuillette, you could say ... as I gather it is that the youths do ... we're just hangin' ...

(a pause as the other tries to understand ...)

two: ... ?! ... oh ... is it that we are a sybil? ... hanging ... sorry, hangin' ... in a glass jar at Cumae ? ...
one: ... nietski, my little orb ... *we* ... are hanging around in ova, as it goes ... we're evolving, baby ...
two: ... ? ... but why? ...
one: ... to metamorphose, natürlich ...
two: ... oh good ... and good-o ... into a butterfly?
one: ... niente, not in the first instance, no ...
two: ... ? ... are we then a pokemon card? ...
one: ... sorry again, sweet pea ... *(reflects)* ... but that might not, to be fair, have been a bad conceit ... for any futural referentialisms ...
two: ... hah! ... I know! ... we are going to be a beetle ... a giant Kafka's beetle! ...
one: ... we-e-e-ll, you *are* getting warmer ... aber nein ... I'm afraid it's more like we're evolving into larvae ... from the Latin, kiddo: larva, larvae first declension, feminine ... meaning ghost, spectre, *evil* spirit ... *horrific* mask ...
two: ... oh dear ... that does *not* sound like a very becoming thing to be becoming ...
one: ... do not to worry yourself, petal ... *(all in one breath)* ... it is merely one of an infinite possible number of representational devices for the ineluctable katachretic modality of written being ... *(nearly expiring as breath is used up)* ... phew(!) ...

two: *(paying no attention to the other's plight)* ... aha! ... *now* I do see ... *we* are a rubbish metaphor ...

one: ... you got it, baby ! ...

two: *(pleased with itself)* ... a meta-phor-mosis (!) ...

one: ... damn straight ... but *I'll* do the jokes around here, thank you kindly ... coolio, though, n'est pas? ... I'm pretty super jolly well pleased with it, really ... given the wraithy relation of word to thing ... the old soft-shoe-shuffle from signifier to signified ... and all the rest of that *blah, blah, blah* ....

two: ... um and hmmmm ... I will refrain from comment here ... where it is we are most presently hanging ...

one: ... humph ... well ... harrumph ... humph again and encore ... that is quite a bit grudging, franchement ... didn't exactly see *you* coming up with anything better in the multiple diverse incarnations and evolutions we have attempted over a not insignificant number of decades ...

two: ... !? ...

(a brief silence ensues in which an attentive reader might just discern a strange chirring sound)

two: ... psssst ...

one: ... what now? ... I'm somewhat rather busy with this changing-state-process, at this instant, currently ...

two: ... how ... *how* ... do we do that? ...

one: ... we eclose ...

two: ... we what ??? ...

one: ... eclose, *Eclose*, ECLOSE! for your life, baby ...

two: ... *ouch* ... no need to shout ...

one: ... in short, we get the hell outta here ... we invert, involute - en effet - we turn inside out ...? ... or is it outside-in?...

two: *(peering out)* ... well, I'm not sure I want to at all be doing that, actually ... not at all ... really *not*, in fact ... it's quite small and safe and cosy in here and out there ... *(peers out again and shivers)* ... is so vasty blank ... and vast ...

one: ... ain't got no choice, ma graine de pavote ... force of nature 'n all, we're an egg - we gotta hatch ... 's the way of the world ... gotta get over and function in the field of language or wir'r ... d-o-o-med ...

two: *(voice quivering)* ... well I'm too scared ... and in fact frightened ... there's nothing out there ...

one: ... not exactly true, little thistle spittle, *ex nihilo nihil fit*, as Parmenides would observe were he here ... *(thinks then adds)* ... and indeed did ... just get out and start crunching away at all that white paper ...

two: *(woozy)* ... !?! ... I don't feel very well ... not very well at all ... oh w-o-e is me! ... I am ... a ... nuance ...

(in which eclosion occurs and we turn away for it is rather indecent to look upon. This big bang is offered alternatively for your viewing pleasure ...)

one: *(dusting self down)* ... well ... that took not a little effort ...

two: *(looking round, catches sight of something at the very periphery, the vanishing point of vision, recoils in fear and horror)* ... YIKES! ... wha-at-s that? ...

one: *(raising one eye and goggling over the rim of a battered pair of reading glasses, unconcerned)* ... oh that ... *that* is an exuvium ... a husk and formless ruin of obsolescence ... *that*, ma chouette chenillette, is our MMOPP, or MOP for ease and speed of appellation ...

two: ... our *what?* ...

one: *(coughs)* ... hem, hem ... our Material Means of Poetic Production ...

two: *(eyeing it up and down)* ... oh ... it doesn't look very nice ...

one: ... no, it doesn't does it? ... in truth, it's *thoroughly* repulsive ... and furthermore, whatever promise it may have had in its youth ... to which, I might add, it has so doggedly failed to live up ... it has now grown o-l-d ... and bitter ...

two: *(turns away, only to start again in shock and horror)* ... well, if that's our MOP, what! ... is ... *that?* ...

one: *(reading glasses fall off as it swivels to see)* ... ah, yes ... well now, that, my sweet, mine own, my pet ... is the GAIa ... *that* is the psychic remnant, the representation of the vicissitudinous pulsing of the void behind the veil, or the skull beneath the skin, if you prefer, with which, as Eliot tells us, Webster was much possessed ... that, tout court is ... *us* ... *(pauses to consider)* ... although in our case, it must be said, we are exo rather than endo ...

two: *(boggled)* ... exo what? ...

one: ... oh *do* try to keep up, popplette, exo-skeletal, évidement ...

two: *(shaking head, disconsolate)* ... dear, oh dear, oh dear, oh dear ... *we* don't look very nice, either ... what *is* a GAIa? ...

one: ... a GAIa, dear heart, is a Governing Authorial Intention ... *(coughs again, mumbling, embarassed)* ... hem, hem .. actually ...

two: ... ACTUALLY?? ...

one: *(somewhat apologetic)* ... yes, yes I know ... you have me banged to rights ... I must, in the interest of full disclosure, concede, that the actually is a bit unnecessary ... but a GAIa has *so* much more sex appeal than a GAI ... dontcha think? ...

... (which indicates a short pause, before ...)

two: ... what I think ... *(falters)* ... what I think ... *(still at a loss)* ... what I think ... is ... *(then)* ... what *I* think is that I need a drink ...

one: ... *I* do not demur, indeed I concur ... it is, in a realistic appraisal of our situational situation ... more simply put, the sitch ... highly likely that something in the superhuge-number-range of drinks will necessarily have to be imbibibulated before this pro-ject has landed on its envers ... its other side ...

two: *(cheered)* ... then let's go and sit down under that bar over there, it's too vasty blank out here by our ownlinesses ...

one: ... d'accord, ma chère cossettinette ... you bring the bag, I'll bring the botts and we will sit ourselves upon the ground and tell sad stories of the death of kings ...

two: ... if it's anything like all your other stuff there'll be no stories, no ground, and no kings either ... *(adds)* ... but sad deaths enough for *any* customer ...

one: *(a little tetchy)* ... well, you can't always get what you want, baby ... come on ...

two: *(grumbling and muttering under its breath)* ... "you bring the bag, yadda, yadda"... I always get the bloody bag ... *(dragging behind the horrific mask of its larval form a battered old leather bag, bulging and splitting at the seams)* ... do we need all these bloody books ... so many, *so* heavy books ... *(louder so the other can hear)* ... do we need all these books ... I'm only quite small and little, you know ...

one: *(looking behind, unmoved)* ... 'fraid so, my tiny chirrup, the books are all we've got to eat ... 'n I hate to break it to you, but not only are you only little and small, you are also ... *(coughs again)* ... hem, hem ... not-at-all ...

two: *(sinks to the ground)* ... that's a bit of a blow, actually, in fact ... *(then, more optimistically)* ... at least there would appear to be ground upon which to sink ...

one: ... yes, apopros of our state of non-being you have my sympathy ... best not dwell on it ... *(offers the bottle)* ... here ... have a slug on that ...

two: *(takes the bottle and swigs)* ... so ... to sum up the state-of-play, or, as you do say, the sitch: we are a GAIa with a MOP ...

one: ... yeppo aleppo, you got it sweetie ... and we are also the first INSTAR of our entomological allegory ...

two: *(reflects)* ... oh, so we've gone from metaphor to allegory ...

one: ... ah yes indeedio ... we've gone up in the world ... figuratively speaking ...

two: *(splutters some drink out)* ... is that supposed to be *funny* ...

one: *(ignoring this)* ... in summary, my nebeneinander ... we are on our way to being a **very** hungry caterpillar ... *(adds)* ... hence all those books ...
two: *(collapses, groaning)* ...
one: *(tuts and shakes its head)* ... tch, tch, tch ... some entities have so little stamina for existential indeterminacy these days ...

(which is the end of the first scene of this drama, which is neither a scene nor a drama. Forgive it – it knows not what it does. The turning of the page is entirely in your hands, gentle reader – but, and this constitutes a warning on behalf of public health and safety: ... ou pire – it only gets worse ...)

Part I

Writing

ΑΝΤΙΓΟΝΕ

(or stuff from the shed)

FREUD: "Was will das Weib?"

ISMHNH: "ἀλλ᾽ ἀμεχάνων ἐρᾷς"

LACAN: "que peut être un tel désir, le désir de l'analyste ? . . .
Dès maintenant, nous pouvons tout de même dire ce
q'il ne peu pas être. Il ne peut pas désirer
l'impossible. "

APOLLO 13: "Houston, we . . . have a problem " (!?)

(ἀμεχάνων = lost in space)

book

and what of the wretched book, my love
that never could be writ
do we concede the truth my love
and make our peace with it?

there are too many words in the world, my sweet
but none are left for me -
I am losing my hold on words my love
they are slipping away from me …

                  oh - must we always fail in the mirror
                  all our noblest houses fall
                  gouge our body contours
                  though no thing stands at all?

I am left with a hole in the wind, my love
a hollow tug of the sea
a tear in the texture of night, my love
a burning I cannot be -

and the bones that break through the skin, my love
and the skin that brazes the bone
and the blood that glozes the brain my love
and the brain that grazes the stone.

                - and so what of a hole and a tug and a tear
                  a burning that can't be borne
                  and what of the bone and the skin and the brain
                  this body that can't be worn?

will a burning braid with the bone, my love
see these hands that are quite blind -
will the brain be hemmed to a hole in the wind
by this bloody skein of mind?

and the skin will be stitched to the tug in the sea
and the stone to the tear in the night
and what ever is made in this way, my love
is all that I can write.

(for Claire and Bernard, in love and squalor)

thread

pot

Plant your head in a pot, my love | and grow quite
twelve feet tall | train your knees to raspberry cane |
or lean against the wall. | | The earth will teach you
well, my love | what never can be said | that deep black
earth you breathe, my love | is how to feed your head.
| | And when you are quite mad, my love | not any
human shape | take your head from the pot, my love |
and see the wise men gape. jx

Is this you, my most marvelous friend? Cx

... hem, hem ... cough, cough ... splutter ... (might be) ...
jx

You - are very, very, very, very good. To the power of
the loop. Cx

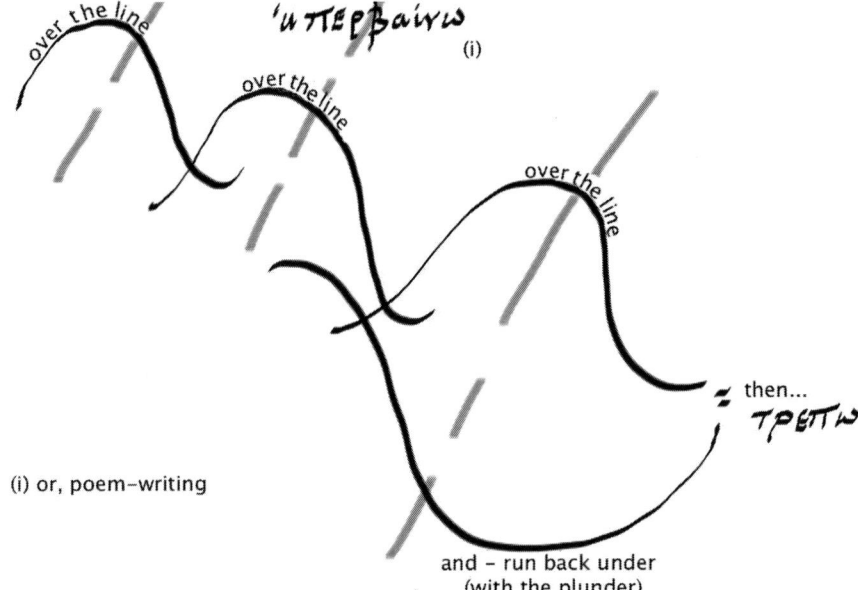

over the line

'υπερβαίνω

(i)

over the line

over the line

then...

τρεπω

(i) or, poem-writing

and – run back under
(with the plunder)

Dear Judith,

You asked me to find a matheme that rendered the impossibility of being both a mother and a writer – this is the one I have come up with:

M: (H2 à H3) | W: (H3 à H2).

The "|" is a sign very beloved of C S Peirce: it stands for "not both" [you can produce all of the beginnings of logic with it]. The French has actually been inserted automatically by transposing the script from Word – I think it works though. The Hs are two of the three kinds of space that I talked about at the Tate. H2 spaces have neighbourhoods containing points where each locality has edge points; the Mother directs the child away from them, so that the child can take a position in the world of the men. The Writer reintroduces the edge points.

I hope the diacritics work in transmission.

dear Bernard,

It is a pretty decisive action, surely, when translating The Iliad, to determine whether to cast the first word as Sing or Rage from the opening μῆνιν ἄειδε. I oscillate, depending on the prevailing configuration of my ψυχή . . . before receiving this, today's translation would definitely have opened on the RAGE side of the question. You can see, now, that the mind has been changed and moved its position. SING! is how we begin. Thank you for that restructuring interpretation . . .

eleven ways of writing not-writing-writing

i. (non) compos mentis

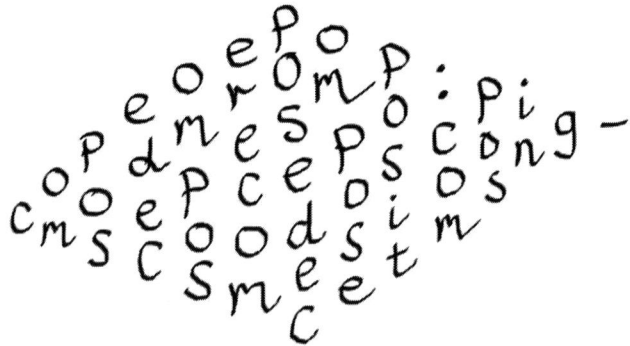

ii. scraping

word bits from the
bottom of the barrel
(having voided said
of its contents)

iii. sloughing

dead skin from the
salt scrolls of the feet

waste writing:
what else?

iv. caught in the act

of burying
something, or digging
something
up
in/from a ditch
X - marks the spot

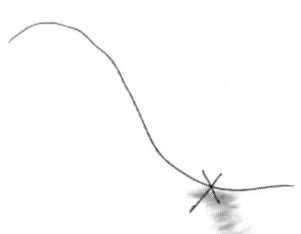

v. der Augenblick

the moment when -

where (are) poems ~~are~~ written in

and ~~but~~ how do they stay still (?)

vi. for paper and ink

flay the skin
stretch it over the w/hole of the world
leave to be weathered
and parched
into parchment

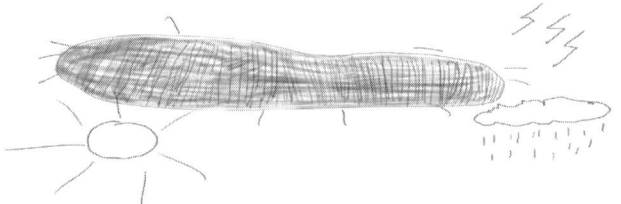

that: is your paper

take the internal organs
their water and their blood

put in a mortar
pound/crunch/pestle
into
a paste

that: is your ink

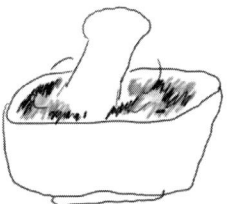

vii. if

we wait
and do not ask
will it come
will it come

if -

no

so… come … come …
come … little letters
come - there, there -
that's the way -
… that's it, good little
letters … come …

viii. vortex

to the core of the earth
there sits a woman, far alone
can she hear her

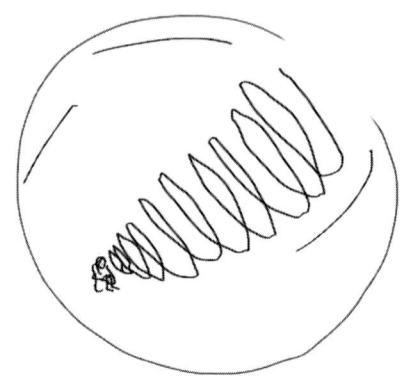

"form -

please find m
please,
form - ?"

ix. braid

- the book
is the braiding
of my daughter's hair

oh, jerusalem

my daughter's hair

for she is comely -

x. why?

- : for it cannot be only of body
it must - l-e-a-p - upon the shelf
to royally fuck all other books
and give birth to itself

be the book
- ah -
be the book
- mmmmm -
be the book -
- oo - again -

xi. non compos mentis (encore)

encore, encore - jg

stone and story

Stone came first
and all and only.
Stone was there
still
and alone.

Then came air
- a breath -
just briefly
and strange : -
there came forth
stone
from stone.

That stone
- inspired -
gave birth to story.
Stone of story
begot by air.
Then story sensed
its own potential
and made a way
away from there.

So dis-encumbered

story spun

and from itself drew one

from one : -

then two, three, four -

near exponential

infinitely

referential.

I have words and you have silence

Story sung to silent stone.

Stone,

old stone,

again

alone

said nothing.

(for Bernard and his book, spring 2010)

love

Second INSTAR

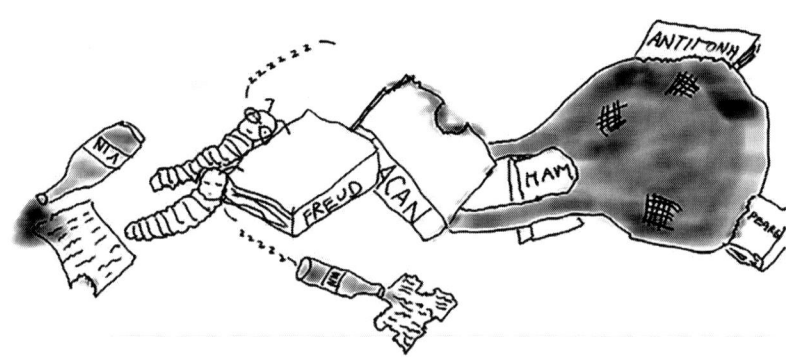

one: *(snoring)* ... zzzzzzzzzzzzzzzzzz ...

two: *(snuffling in sleep)* ...
bibblesnifflezzzzzzzzzbabblesnofflezzzzzzzzzbubblesnibblezzzzzzzz ...

one: *(waking groggy)* ... whooah ... where am I? ...

two: *(moaning)* ... oh, wo-e is me, o-h ... I do not feel, in fact, too very well,
actually ...

one: *(gingerly)* ... no, I am, I fear, also not entirely compos mentis ... indeed, it
would be fair and not a great distance from the truth to observe that *we* ... are
drunk ... *(declaiming grandly)* ... *drunk* like Dionysus ...

two: *(groaning)* ... drunk, for surely sure ... but like Dionysus ... really ... I do, in
fact, wonder ... *(looking down at itself)* unless he too actually did assume grotesque
larval form ...

one: *(thinks)* ... wouldn't have put it past him ... now you mention it ... *(then
warming to the sound of its own voice)* ... drunk it is that indeed we are ... *drunk* ... like
the Persians of Herodotus ...

two: ... !? ...

(there is an interval in which both fall back to sleep, hence)

one: *(snoring again)* ... zzzzzzzz ...

two: *(snuffling, rather tunefully, in sleep)* ... zzzzzbabblefobblesniffleboфflezzzzzzzzz
...

one: *(wakes, surprising itself again)* ... aha! ... here we still seem to be are then
(looking out over wonky reading glasses, nudges the other to wake it up) ...

two: *(disgruntled)* ... wha-a-at? ... oh ... it's *you* ... what do *you* want? ...

one: ... any comment? ... my somewhat grumpling umbel ...

two: ... any comment on *what?* ...

one: *(impatient)* ... on the preceeding preceedings, obviously, my plumping dumpling ...

two: ... no ...

one: ... oh ...

two: *(then takes some time to reflect)* ... well, actually, yes ... in actual fact ...

one: ... what? ...

two: ... well, I was wondering why it is that it is ... all so ... *(searches for a term which is not too impolitic)* ...

one: *(a little defensive)* ... why it is that it is all so ... so *what?* ... exactly ...

two: *(hesitant)* ... all so ... *odd* ... odd and peculiar ... and peculiarly odd ...

one: ... ah, is that all? ... it is because, my milkweedy sweetling ... if you consider the multimeta- nay, near pata-phoric entities it is that we are ... how? ... *(expansive and knocking glasses entirely askew)* ... I ask **HOW**? could a prosaic linear linguistic offering possibly encompass and convey ... let alone commune with the impossibile infinitude of possibilities it is that it is that we are???? ...

two: *(wincing)* ... *aieeee* ... would you *please* to keep the noise level down ...

one: ... bien sùr ... ma bête en boulette ... I do understand ... you have, what Oofy Prosser of the Drones would term, a morning head ... now, where was I ... ? ... ah, yes ... *(continues declaiming, now in a stage whisper)* ... only a very narrow, mono-directional mind could be satisfied or sustained by the railway track potentiality of your workaday single-dimensional sentence ...

two: ... ok, ok, I get it ... pass the bott would you ...

one: *(screwing a new top off and handing it over)* ... here you go, kiddo ... and also ... as the old music-hall standard goes: ... *(now singing con gusto)* ... *"for only the oddest live at the edges/ and most of the oddest are mad, are mad/ and all of the oddest are mad/ and all of the oddest/ and all of the oddest/ and **all** of the oddest - are mad"* ... sing along if the mood takes you, little pod ...

two: *(suspicious)* ... what old music-hall standard in fact is that? ... exactly ...

one: *(insouciant)* ... well, truth be told ... and truthfully ... one I just made up ... catchy, though ... n'est ce pas? ...

two: *(suddenly vertiginous)* ... oh no ... here it goes again ...

one: ... who-a-h ... age cannot wither ... nor custom stain ...

two: ... our infinite ... meta .. phor ... icity ...

one: ... that's not sooo bad, as it ... go-o-o-o-o- -o- -e --s ...

(you are asked please to look away again, dear reader, as grotesque skin sloughing is in the process of occurrence ... you may wish to turn the page, by way of a diversion. Then again, you may not. Perhaps the best course of action would be to get it over with quickly: if t'were done, when t'is done, then t'were best t'were done rapidamente and all that ...)

Part II Lost

thread/hospital

Most relevant, I have managed to finish your poem.
I will bring it to the (hush, hush and on the QT)
hospital, love judithgracielivesinabucket x

My finger. Your toe. A pebble. Never doubt. Cx

. . . .

. . . .

. . . .

Oh dear. Oh dear. The kitchen closed. No cup of
tea and they made me wait for more than an hour
for pain relief and a bed pan and all other indignities
to which flesh is heir etc, etc and I had to have a row
with the nurse and I cried and. and. And. But. Well.
So. (as my sensai Claire would have and did say). But
I'm all right now, baby it's an a-l-r-i-ght now. And
we are AMAZING and you looked too beautiful
for worlds today and that made my soul soar. Sleep
the sleep of the good honest sinners, darlingest.
Love (shhhhhhh whisper only to the baby mice that
scutter in your skirting boards) itwouldappearthat
judithgraciereallydoeslivehere xxxxxxxx

Judith. You are in my hand. Cx

Thank you so. Oh so, my Claire. I think you are an
angel not very heavily disguised. judithmutilategra-
ciefallsasleepinherbucketwithadonkeysmileuponher-
bustedbust x

No cause. No cause. Sparkle, you do. Yoda syntax.
Cx

Particle wavelengths. Special silver PARTICLE
wavelengths. The finest filigree silver threads woven
across the intergalactic way of nut, love judithgra-
cieonthecaseofspace x

. . . .

. . . .

. . . .

Claire. Oh Claire. I need the touch of your mind
by text. I am adrift in hostile waters with no instru-
ments. Pray. In earnest. jx

All my soul is with you. Darling. Their breakdown
has already happened. Put it away from you, if you
can. Your silver strands are all still there, shimmer-
ing across the darkness of the void. And Judith
Gracie is your wonderful name. Cx

. . . .

. . . .

. . . .

Oh. Oh. Oh. It won't do. Fuckerama. As my sensai,
guru, master, professor, philosopher, Claire, has
been heard to observe on occasion. Under the
painted porch on Mondays, or the bodhi tree on
Tuesdays. Strolling along Eleatic shores every second Sunday ... and in a shaded corner of the agora
on Wednesdays and Fridays. Today, which is the day
after what was the yesterday, they have instituted
a new policy in the hospital that gives nurses the
authority to eject those visitors who are a danger to
the patient whom they are (what is called) visiting
(!?). Too late for me. Eheu. Alack. Aiee, aiee – jx

Do not forgive them, for they know exactly what they do. Ah, the rain it raineth every day . . . Cx

Raineth!?! pelteth/smiteth/blasteth/battereth/ striketh/bombardeth/assaileth/hurleth and all other verbeths of violent assault : -
love judithgracie'sexistentialcontinuityhangsinthebala nceinherbatteredbucket xxxxx

And another thing. They don't like it up 'em. Cx

I LOVE you, Claire. At such a volume that all the neighbours are complaining about the noise and I have not even opened my mouth ... yet, jx

Dear heart. Your mind when I hear it speak to mine makes me laugh. When the only jokes are utterly appalling. Cx

. . . .

. . . .

. . . .

Home. With smokes and three gins in. And surely let us speak upon the morrow though I cannot guar- antee that any recognizable language will come out of the mouth of judithgracieismynameandIlivein- abucketofginandtonic xxxxx

Home. My loveliness. Oh what a colossal thing you have done, out on a planet of wild desolation with huge knives. I will very much want to speak in the morning. I love you woman. Cx

I send this to inform you that judithgraciewholives-
inabucketetc sent Bernard a drunken email about
the Persians of Herodotus and she is not sure if she
is even sorry. WHO can she think it is that she is????
I ask you? jx

You honour Bernard with drunken email ... he will
know that. Cx

"Raise high the roofbeam, carpenters. Like Ares
comes the bridegroom, taller far than a tall man."
That's you, that is - jx

. . . .

. . . .

. . . .

god, oh god

her little brother is dead

he did not go to bed

he killed himself instead

with a belt around his neck

stān   **stone**

stān on stān   stone on stone
bān on bān   bone on bone
bān on blōd   bone on blood
blōd on stān   blood on stone

stān on stān   stone on stone
brægen on brægen   brain on brain
blōd on brægen   blood on brain
brægen on stān   brain on stone

blōd on stān   blood on stone
blōd on bān   blood on bone
brægen on brægen   brain on brain
stān on stān   stone on stone

                                              this
                                         is
                                    as
        - please, please help me now …   near
                                as
                         I
                     can
                 get,
             my
         dear
      x

(for my Claire - oh, Claire - whose little brother has killed himself all away)

two women, naked

two women, naked
lying in the dark
half covered in earth
stretching, hands out, fingers splayed
in the utmost extended effort
to touch
the other's
finger
tip

two women, naked
each
apart
from the other
rolled up into the tightest ball
nearby -
but at odd
not connecting
angles,
sad

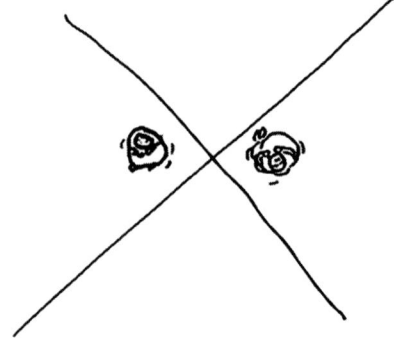

two women, naked
eyes gouged out of both -
black ink,
coming from their
closed mouths
all down the front
of their
forlorn
bodies

two women, naked
face on
one to the other,
holding hands,
smiling
both with a gun
to their
brains

two women, naked
on the very narrowest
of edges
with the deepest drop
of impossible descent
on either side -
most precariously
balanced
by their taking
of the other's
weight

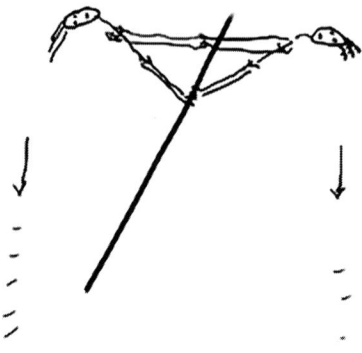

two women, naked
one kneeling,
hands and arms extended
tired,
an uncomfortable position
the other
lying on her painfully arched back

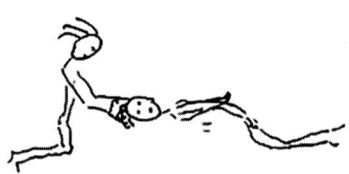

head slightly raised
eyes closed

slightly raised head
and opisthotonic back,
being held
by the extended hands and arms of the
kneeling
other

two women, naked
one is submerged
and drowning
deep
in a tank of water
the other hangs over the edge
necessarily having tethered her foot or ankle
uneasily
to a wooden post on the outside
she is suspended also
deep
in the tank

and,
in what appears to be a kiss,
delivers a mouthful of air
in her breath
to the
drowning
other

(to be continued)

fallen woman

Terror may lurk in a handful of dust,
or the turbinate bones of the nose : -
Hell brood in each grain of Sandymount sand : -
in the worm at the bed of the rose.

But keep her away from the ridges
where the very next step is a fall.
Keep her far, far away from the edges -
- beyond which, there is nothing at all.

For sheer is the
drop
from the cliffs - atop which -
the sibilant siren sings

her song enthralls
the endless
fall
through the nothingness
of things

to Solitude

of such a mortal kind

that mind

no longer

speaks

to mind.

mouth

Third INSTAR

---

two: *(sobbing)* ... sad I am, I am *so* sad ...

one: *(sniffing with reading glasses all steamed up)* ... yes my little rosy, my little rosy pants ... ich auch ... es ist ganz sehr traurig ... wirklich ...

two: ... I do not feel so much that I want to carry on anymore on ... in actual matter of fact ... really ...

one: *(adjusting glasses and looking at the other)* ... no ... it *is* a blow to the being-being-able-to-do-ongoing-of-being ...

two: ... too sad I am ... I am **too** sad to bear ...

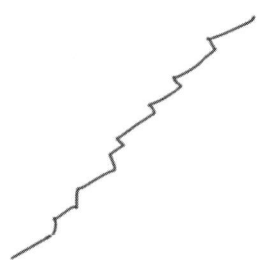

(that ... was a rip in the space-time continuum ...)

(now ...)

one: *(very relieved to be back in speech)* ... ah! ... here it would again appear that we continue to be being ... *(looking down at the still sobbing other)* ... and yes, I am sad also, meine schöne schweinekleine ... the sadness is truthfully and indeed everywhere and all around ubiquitous ... but do remember do, little rosy ... blessèd are they that mourn ... ... for they shall be comforted ... my little rosy pantakins ...

two: ... blessèd be they that mourn ... for they shall be comforted ... *(considers this)* ... that is a nice thing to say ... actually ... and would be if it could in fact be true ...

one: ... ah, but it **is** true, my rosy pantallonables ... but fair yes to say, true only in the hardest and most schmerzlich of ways ... as some French chappie did write down ... it is *impossible* to economize on mourning ...

two: ... you mean you cannot do it on the cheap? ...

one: ... exactemente ...

two: *(adds)* ... or get a BOGOF ...

one: *(appalled)* ... tch,tch,tch ... no BOGOFS in mourning ... tch, tch, tch ... *absolument* **pas** ...

(a pause in which still more sobbing and sniffling sounds can be heard alongside crunching and munching noises ... which might look something like this ... snifflemunchohdearsobmunchsnottlewail ... and also might not ...)

two: *(suddenly)* ... apple tree ... it was apple-tree! ...

one: *(not following)* ... *what* was apple-tree ... my pippin ...

two: ... who writ down that thing what you just did say ...

one: ... ah, ouias! ... main bien sùr que oui ... it was indeed un pommier ... Gerard Pommier ... rosy posy pippini pants ... *(head slowly shaking to and fro in sombre evaluation)* ... and forsooth a good and truly thing that he writ and said ...

(another pause, then ...)

two: *(with a tiny aspiration of hope)* ... I wonder ... I wonder if ...

one: ... what is it that you wonder ... my ampling rosy pantaloons?...

two: ... I wonder if ... if *I* am what can be called rosy pants ... could *you* be ... could you maybe perhaps be called ... *(a little bashful)* ... could you maybe be what might be called ... gildy sperm? ...

one: ... hmmm ... well now, *that* is an interesting proposition, not-so-little rosy ... yes, we could be Gilda Sperm and Rosy Pants ... indeed, yes ... yes, indeed ... an act of nomination ... se faire des noms ... to make of ourselves some names ... yes, yes ... that might work ...

two: ... well, in fact, Rosy Pants and Gildy Sperm would be what is the more technically correct actually ... I do know this for surely sure ... see ... I have only just eaten all of that one nearly all the whole way through ... *(gesturing towards a very well munched and nearly no longer extant copy of Hamlet)* ...

one: ... well, yes ... and fair do's and inkums ... I'd have to take that one on the old chin ...

two: *(pushing)* ... and it *is* a little bit silly and cheerful ...

one: *(struggling to look through its steamed up reading glasses)* ... sans doute, little Rosy, ridiculous and silly and, if I may borrow for a moment your kiasmic trope, *ridiculously* silly names are definitively more cheerful than people going around dying all over the place ... and willy-nilly ...

two: *(happier)* ... have we been and blessèd ourselves in our comforting, then gildy gilda? ...

one: doch aber ja! ... indeed we have, we have indeed ... what a piece of fine work it is that it is that we are, n'est ce pas? nicht wahr? ...

two: *(groaning)* ... aiee, aiee ... Gildy, I think it's happening again ...

one: *(dizzy)* ... yes, Rosy ... blackout! ... heaven ... h-e-e-e-lp ... blazing ...

two: ... aaaargh ... into ... the ... h-e-a-d ...

(once again, we must try your patience dear reader and ask that you avert gaze from another revolting skin-sloughing event (or SSE) ... back before you've had time to miss us. Meanwhile a forward page turning action (FPTA) —> might just be in your interest at this critical juncture. You decide ...)

Part III Tragedy

thread/down

Down these mean streets I must go. Every
moment has been agony - but I couldn't have
done otherwise. Cx

Précise . . . jx

(x , y)

A
Γ
A
M
E
M
On the softest slope, of the rosiest dawn,
before all sorts of other things were born
the two loveliest girls - one dark, one fair -
lay in the happiest tangle, sleeping there -

and their names were Time and Death
and they did not know that yet
M

←——— Ι Φ Ι Γ Ε Ν Ι Α ———→

Ω
N

with this act now
come Time and Death
ἄναξ ἀνδρῶν
Lord of Men.

↓

(for Bernard and his whiteboard: spring 1980 - summer 2013)

trees

i.

I asked the trees to speak to me

But they stayed silent. Not a sound.

Outlawed by madness in the blood,

I looked from far behind my mind

and asked again

round every bend

but nothing came.

ii.

Hung from a twisting fray of thought

I swung; and snatched at thought with sight -

looked out again to the Other world

of old brown autumn leaves turned gold

and on the branch, now wrought in bronze,

a perfect bird alive with song

in the wide blue air of winter sun.

iii.

And I could see that it was good.

But still I could not hear a word.

And as feet went from tree to tree

I felt language - forsaking me.

swerve:

I

- swung

and

fell

iv.

Mind felled. All felled.

Beneath the ground.

Where feet --/--

-- feel -- the ancient contours

of an earthly sound

v

Through the brittle soughing of old, golden leaves

Came the sacred plainsong of the trees : -

" They slew us for the funeral pyre

of little songbird

Ιφιγενια -

We bled our sap and swore back then

never

to speak the words of men.

But you are strange. Not of their kind.

So we chant this κυρια to

your unspun mind. "

vi.

Then feet. Silly feet --- with their metric tread

unearthed the frays and twined the thread.

Set good measure through heliotropic gloom

twitched their mantle

and took me home.

(October 2010 – October 2013)

"εἴθε μὴ ἔφυς

Curse You.

Curse You.

Curse You.

I *damn* you to all hell for our daughter
Dogfaced perversion in the name of father

Winds - was it? Troy - was it? Power and Glory?
Different Proper Noun. Same Old Story.

Know this now.

Here I hurl this oath:

No cosmic quaking will erode my *Fury*."

dear Bernard,

Here, amongst other things, I am trying to formulate the premises for your sigils regarding The Winter's Tale (TWT). And have not known how long or how short this email ought to be. Enfin, I think it is now both far too long and far too short. Which is probably no damn good at all. Anyway. As my grandma used to say: on y va . . .

First sigil.

As we discussed, is the shorthand of all Shakespearean tragedy:

Each man kills the thing that he loves. Why does each man do this?

(by the way, it is masculine insistence that gets the whole thing going: Leontes/ Lear/Creon – they insist and insist and insist and cannot hear anyone else's speech actions. Do you remember telling me how Henry Fonda (?) wanted his ashes to be deposited in the kitchen bin; whoever his poor woman was, she was being insisted on, in her psychic and physical space, even after his death.)

Second sigil.

Having done this, in the sharp switch of genre from tragedy to comedy that occurs in TWT, there is a repudiation of the consequence of action. I think **S** is demonstrating that repudiation of consequence is equivalent to ethical wrong.

(This also speaks to my wider thesis regarding tragedy, i.e. that it is a rigorous tracking of the logical consequence of action and thereby an inherently hopeful enterprise: if x follows from y action, then had there been z action the outcome could/would have been different. This also explains the multidimensionality of tragedy – it wouldn't work if we couldn't conceive of all sorts of other parallel universes where subtly different actions and outcomes could/will are happen/ ing). Ergo, King Lear is a play of promise and possibility. TWT is a play of disillusion, and . . . despair (?)

Third sigil.

Is to do with the ethics of art. There is something obscene about the lifelike statue of Hermione that apparently comes alive at the end of the play. (Though Leontes' and Hermione's seven year old son, Mamillius, is definitively dead, in case we need any orientation). With this totalising artistic reproduction, the dead body of mother and son are left unmourned and unaccounted for.

Browning does something structurally similar in My Last Duchess, though the murdering male speaker there is clearly evil and not (apparently) redeemed – as Leontes would seem to be.

So such art is being used to cover over the gap in the real/to obscure the real consequences of action/to relieve Leontes of moral responsibility, and is thereby a wilful participant in wrongdoing. An agent of the bad side.

This is a very short outline. I ought also to say – in caveat – that I am not a Shakespeare scholar in the universities and my reading of TWT is not, I think, standard. I take responsibility for any misinterpretation.

An afterthought. I think it could be argued that what **S** real-ises in TWT is the end of the Christian god, way before Nietzsche, Darwin or Marx. But that's a story for another day.

I hope this is not unconstructive.

J

Dear Judith,

This morning I found a good motto for our sigils: "The goal was a new and higher *mechane* of existence, the birth of the *tragic thought*"; the italics are Nietzsche's – the phrase is from his "The Dionysiac World-View", written in 1870.

scapegoat

Eventually, they found the scapegoat sleeping tunefully in a bed of dirty straw, on the steep, cobbled wynd behind the stables of the inn. It had clearly just had a meal of cabbage stalks, apple cores and old hunks of bread, for the remains of such was scattered amongst the straw having been purloined from the waste the potboy had lobbed over the hatch earlier that evening. It appeared to be dreaming; as it slept, its rhythmic snoring and wheezing hummed an odd but not altogether unpleasant melody.

One of the watchmen prodded at the scapegoat with his long spear, thereby waking it up.

"Ba-a-a-a," it stuttered, as, startled, the white ear lifted higher than its other black one. Or, if you are able to interpret the strange sounds of scapegoats, something along the lines of, "Uh-oh, here we go again."

"We simply cannot have this creature in the city a moment longer. Really. It's too bad," said the chamberlain to his scribe and attending men. "Look at its depredations. How it eats everything up and then lies around disporting itself in this egregious manner, making its imbecilic facial expressions and these unconscionable noises." He flung his arms wide to emphasize the ubiquity of his argument, and was temporarily distracted by the ermine trimming on his sleeves. "And that is to say nothing of its – ahem – excremental activities. If we permit the situation to persist, it will consume all our resources and we will be unable to feed and shelter those who live legitimately and do an honest day's labour within our city walls. We must persuade the king to take decisive action. For the greater good. Immediately. At all costs. And forthwith. To boot."

His scribe duly noted all of this down in the heavy ledger, which solemn official record bore testament to many not very various thematic variations delivered by the chamberlain, and off they went to put their suit before the king.

The king was in conversation with the queen:

"The neurosis is over," he was saying. "We are all better."

"Oh," responded the queen, who, though he was neither an especially cruel nor especially stupid man for a king, seldom paid much attention to anything he said.

"What do we do now then?" she asked. Still squinting through her eyeglasses at the scroll unrolled on the writing table in front of her.

While the king was pondering a witty and trenchant and, indeed, regal answer to what he admitted to himself was a decent, if insufficiently-fascinated, question on the part of his wife, a din began to be heard clamouring towards their chamber.

"Oh no. It will be the chamberlain come to drone on about the scapegoat again," sighed the king. "I'll have to do something about it this time."

"Why?" queried the queen. Looking up from plans she was working on for a more flexible and efficacious network of defences designed to allow indwellers and travellers to cross in and out of the city more easily while simultaneously enabling protective fortifying devices to be lodged swiftly into position if hostilities threatened.

Hmmm, she never says much but she always has a damn well point, thought the king, but replied instead:

"Because."

And then paused.

"Because … he goes around the whole city from dawn till dusk, muttering darkly to armourers and acrobats, bakers and brewers, coopers and, and – and c - - "

"Cartwrights," suggested the queen. "Ditchers and dyers, ewers, engravers, farriers and fletchers?" she went on.

"Yes. Well. To all the people," said the king with a hint of irritation. "Stirring discontent and division up and down. High and low. We'll have to get rid of the scapegoat this time."

He paused again. Rubbed his hand over his face. And added:

"It won't be such a tragedy."

The queen looked up again from her parchment. Stuck her quill into her elaborate coiffure causing an inkblot to arc across her cheek in, so the king thought, anyway, a deliciously fetching manner.

"Bit of a tragedy for the scapegoat, though. One could say.

You might want to think about the consequences, dear."

And went back to her plans.

Just then, three perfunctory raps shook the door of their chamber. The king rolled his eyes at the rafters. Which were less responsive than the queen.

"Perhaps I was somewhat premature," he said "about the neurosis, I mean."

"here we go again ...."

etched I

"All men kill the thing they love . . . and outcasts always mourn."

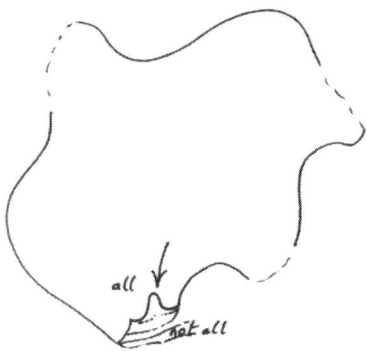

Boundaries are crossed in a variety of circumstances; at times however, they are rendered fixed. When they contain and bound a privileged space – particularly an ideally privileged space – those on the other side suffer a genocidal hate.

bb

ballad of the stupid feet

She wandered in the wilderness
and stubbed her feet on stone.
She said: "These feet are stupid.
It's time that I went home."

But when she broached the city walls
they would not let her in.
They said "Your speech sounds mad to us.
Your body reeks of sin."

She sat down in the dust. She wept.
For forty days and nights.
Her broken toes were bleeding,
her skin ruddled with blight.

And just when Hope was hopeless,
a noise chirred in her head.
A sound she'd never heard before -
word-bits no one else had said.

And then her broken, bleeding feet
began to dance around.
And as she spun with arms outflung
the blood etched in the ground.

The burghers on the battlements
looked over and they read
that writing writ in blood and dance
harrowed them with dread.

"Well, should we let her in?" they asked
"this woman kind of thing.
Could we purge those awful feet?
And douse the stench of sin?"

But as they called their quorum
to talk the matter out,
the object of their counsel
had turned herself about.

And gone back to the wilderness
of tree, of bind, and stone -
to forage her own footpaths
through earth as yet unknown.

And as she stumbled further on
past rock and blasted tree,
she heard a thrumm - a sprung rhythm -
and thought - "that sounds like me."

And Lo. It was a crookèd hut.
And a crookèd kind of crone
who sat and smoked a crookèd pipe
carved from a crookèd kind of bone.

So she sat and passed the time there
and smoked the pipe of bone.
She thought "I am of the wilderness.
But I am not alone."

And with that blaze of blessing -
that truth as true as song -
she bundled up her burdens
and she skipped her way along.

(For Claire and Bernard, Christmas 2005, as it goes)

crones

Three old crones
upon their stones
casting runes
and reading bones.

Hunched outside the city walls,
unseen, unwelcome to them all,
where from their obscene edge of things
they mind the sleep of those within.

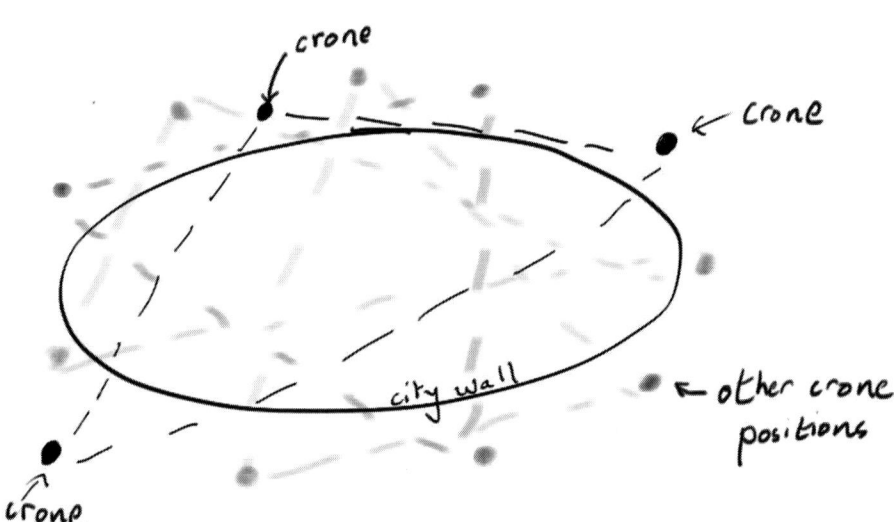

pray

Fourth (of these fine) INSTARS

one: ... well, well, welly my not insubstantial rosy pantaloonikins, what do we make to all that then? ...

two: *(pauses)* ... in truthly, I didn't mind that so very much ... at least it had some paciness ...

one: ... really! ... good, good, and most excellent ... and super amazing ... because *(coughs and tries to locate reading glasses which are now precariously dangling on the slant)* ... because ... hem, hem ... I rather fear the next stuff will bury us alive ... or indeed, dead ... in kthonic gloom ...

two: *(deflated)* ... oh, that's a bit of a downer ... to be coming up ...

one: ... how almost Heraclitian is your observation, bumpling ... yes, a literal kata/strophe ... here ... *(cracking open another bottle and offering it)* ... have a slug, my rumpling sumpling ...

two: *(drinking deeply)* ... gildy? ...

one: ... ya, meine-nicht-so-kleine? ...

two: ... if we **are** a GAIa ... as you did actually once in fact say ...

one: ... I did, I did ... indeed we are, we are indeed ...

two: ... well then ... why don't we know what in fact we are going to be doing exactly next, actually? ...

one: ... splendid, molto splendidio ... my roly poly rosy ... now this dialectic is *really* setting the heather on fire ... *(breathes in, before embarking on explanation)* ... I think, my lumpling lieblung, that as GAIas go, we are in the nature of being more of a nachträglich kind of GAIa ...

two: ... oh ... what *is* that ? ... what you do call a nachträglich kind of GAIa, gildy ? ...

one: *(pauses)* ... w-e-l-l ... it is, I think, fair to say for the starting starters ... and firstly ... that *all* acts of language ... which it forsoothly has to be said that we are ... and indeed representations of cultural representation ... must by definition be afterwards ... ma pétallette rose ...

two: ... after what? ...

one: ... after the endlessly elusive non-knowable *living* moment, pod ... the ontologigorical *being* of the thing ... it's the inbuilt upfucked nature of the system ... you can never say what it *is* that the *is is* ... toss the coin and take your pick between the old chaudron or the cloche ... both malheureusement, tout à fait ... *fêlé/e* ...

two: *(not understanding)* ... but I do not know this what and what it is between, gildy ... that you do tell me to be taking the pick of ...

one: ... your Flaubert or your Baudelaire, my flabulosi farfallulla ... to wit: some muckle great umbel-shaped utensil shot through with a big botch of a crack ... *(breathes in deeply before further hammed-up exclamation)* ... some man-made artyfactual representative representation of the original ur-belly ... which is, of course ... your predictable and proverbial ur-Mother ... the originatrix of all ungodly grendels from the ur-swamp ... and yet, and yet ... said busted old barrel (of an) organ ... is all we've got to sing out our immortal souls, my blot, my splot, my broken pot ... inshallah ... world without end ... et cetera ... et cetera ... et cetera ... young grasshopper ...

(the other digests this, along with several pages, then ...)

two: ... oh, I think I *do* see ... so ... what you are saying ... *(reflects again)* ... is that language entities of words and suchlike stuff ... that as you say it is that it is that we are ... are all ... a kind of *elegaic* type of entity ...

one: ... bingo! ... straight to the point ... the heart of the matter ... and indeed well-said ... meine Größe rosa Raupe ... you hit the old target squarely on its bonce ...

two: ... and if that is so, gildy ... would it be a thing to say that writing-type entities ... such as our very and goodly selves, actually ... are a sort of ... also, as well ... entombment ... of the more living-being-thing-of-speaking-speech-straight-out-of-body-and-belly-with-voice-of-breath, in fact ... ? ... *(slumps with* *the exertion of such an excessively-but-necessarily-compounded-noun)* ...

one: *(delighted with the other's thought)* ... ha! ... indeed yes, oh yes indeed ... and as you like to say, mia rosa bella ... for *surely* sure ... writing as ἐπιτάφιος of speech ... how delicious and infinitely loopy and *délicieux* is such an inter-meshing-referential netting, ma pousse ... good ... and good ... e molto bene ...

two: *(now recovered and basking in such approval ... keen for more)* ... is there any more to say about this question of the GAIa that we are then, gildy ...

one: ... oh, indeed, and yes indeediolo ... I could go on for ever and ever and on with variations on this particular and especial and most favourite of all the themes ...

two: ... do ... *do* go on then ...

one: ... alors, and so secundo ... furthermore and moreover ... if we knew exactly what we were going to be or do ... before we did *be* the being or *do* the doing ... we would learn nothing of ourselves, or anything else ... which would be a bit dull and st-u-p-i-d, do you not agree? ...

two: *(somewhat uncertain)* ... I suppose so ...

one: *(carries on with its argument)* ... as those antique Greeks were so very fond of saying ... my humpling chumpling ... παθεῖν μαθεῖν ...

two: *(none the wiser)*... παθεῖν ... μαθεῖν ... what is that? ...

one: ... it is that ... to suffer is to learn, ma gousse ... *(thinks a little)* ... we only learn anything *after* enduring through the brutal-suffering which is lived-experience ... and the knowledge learnt through such enduring ... my portling peapod ... is ... *(searches for an adjective)* ... well, it is ... *appalling* ... and will leave such a mark, a limp, a stain, a scar upon us ... *(drops voice to a very low and solemn tone)* ... that we can never ever ... never ever and not ever ... be the same ... *ever* again ...

two: *(downcast)* ... that is *not*, in fact, sounding so much like a hoot and a toot and a riot of fun and japely-jinks, actually ...

one: ... no indeed ... the busted barrel-organ being of the body's not always ... nay ... is rarely ... full of the belliest of laughs ... which is why no one, as it goes ... *yeeeeuuuuch* ... in the sensible sense of stolid self-interested defensive operations and pugilisms ... wants *anything* to do with it ... and why ... ergo, en plus and therefore ... so many ... most all, in truth ... do repudiate the παθεῖν/ μαθεῖν ... the pity of it all ... the lacrimae rerum ... and do choose *not* to learn anything ... not anything at all ... *(adds, as a quiet afterthought)* ... making them pretty very damn well terrorising dangerous for the other entities around and about ... 'm afraid to say ... which is a shame, frankly ...

(there is a short silence ...)

two: *(has been pondering deeply while the other spoke)*... if we *are* a nachträglich kind of GAIa, gildy ... which it would seem to be that we are ... then is it that most anything that we do *do* as a GAIa is ok to be doing, gildy gilda? ... because if I have understood you rightly and correct ... it would seem that we somewhat, in fact, do make it up for ourselves afterwards actually ... and so can write it out and about any-old-which-way-how that we want ...

one: ... tch, tch, tch ... and pshaw ... oh no, no, no, no, no ... and no ... negativo ... and in the negative ... *(then pauses and qualifies its emphasis)* ... though you are entirely right and present and correct in one sense, my rosalettabêtta ... any symbolic system ... as you do infer ... is open to such wilful manipulation and abuse ... but that *we* are by way of being a nachträglich GAIa does **not** mean anything goes ... my rosiest of all dimpling dawns ... otherwise ... as your question so astutely implied ... all's just wars and lechery ... the whole goddamn time ... and nothing else holds fashion ...

two: ... but if anything does not go just as well and anyhow, gildy ... what then else is there though, gildy gilda? ...

one: ... ah ... well, yes ... my rosy posy pattakin cattikin ... the *else* ... is Aeschylus' blunt offering Δρασαντι παθειν ... or the deed-doer must bloody well pay ... the tragic ethic of consequence ... which is, as it goes, the lodestone of the limit which is law and counterwise the law which is limit ... thusly and adunque ... the foundational necessity of any settled settlement ... all your communal space-sharing configurations, pod, from trogloditious cave dwellers onwards, poddinetski ...

two: ... *(not quite following)* ... but *how* is that so and meaning what, gildy? ...

one: ... well, you can't be allowed to go around killing people all over the shop, any-so-which-way-how ... as *you* would say ... that the mood grabs you ... it's just not cricket ... a responsible GAIa must engage in a rigorous and perpetual inscription and reinscription of what would seem to have been and happened ...

two: *(a bit mindblown)* ... jeepers ... and in fact gee whizz ... actually ...

one: *(continuing on its theme, now intoning in a rather pompous pedagogic manner)* ... and what is furthermore, moreover and additionally ... an endless looping intrication of consequential thought-effort must be undertaken with regard to the question of what is and what is not going to be done, or thought or said upcomingly ... *(shaking now very heavy head to and fro with gravitas)* ... or properly bad things will, do be ... and indeed are happening ... all over the place and everywhere ... all of the time ... so be it ... as it is said and writ ... in perpetuam rei memoriam ...

two: ... *ooooof* ... and phew ... that sounds a bit very much like a hard work of hard labour ...

one: ... 'fraid so, kiddo ... *(breaking into song)* ... " 's a hard ... 's a hard ... it's a ha-ha-ha-hard ... it's a ... h-a-r-d rain ... that's gonna f-a-a-a ..."

two: ... do you mean like that Creon personage, gildy ... spending ages making speeches of quite a long and considerable length and duration ... *then* doing the burial rites he had gone so mental crazy and crazy mentalist about not such a long time previous ... *before* going to get Antigone out of the tomb into which he *himself* actually had in fact put her ... *that* one ... *(glowering at the holey and well-munched copy of* Antigone *protruding from the battered bag)* ... left a *not* pleasant taste in the mouth, actually and in matter of factually ...

one: ... précise ... précise ... indeed ... *"c'est pire qu'un crime, c'est une faute"* ... as Napoleon's chief of police observed, regarding the murder of the Duc d'Enghien ... which happens to be a pretty good working definition of such tragic hamartia as that to which you do so well and so appositely to refer**,** my pinkling flumpling ...

two: *(squirming)* ... Creon ... he for surely sure has room for improvement but just keeps getting worse and worse and worser ... all the way to the end ... it made me come over all itchy and quite scratchy and not so very well feeling ...

one: ... yes, that is another, thirdly and tertium aspect of nachträglichkeit ... and indeed the strong point well made by Solon of Athens when he goes visiting with that rich-as-and-quite-smugly-Croesus ... you can't tell whether a thing's had a *good* life shape of things, until the endpoint of it ...

two: ... and ... but ... well ... what is so very much to speak about that, gildy? ...

one: ... hmmm ... take us, say, for example ... or indeed, if you prefer ... consider the larvae of the leaf ... we are not currently or at the moment the most pulchritudinous of entities, or at least, conventional estimatation of larval incarnation is not that it is of the optimal aesthetic ... but with all this formal shapeshifting we undergo ... who can know how we will end up when we put the stop at the end of the multiplicity of this sentence that it would seem to be that we are in for? ...

two: *(brighter)* ... ah, you mean things, or the sitch as you do like to say, may still have room for improvement ... or oppositely round ...

one: *(shudders)* ... yes, trust me, rosy posy pattacake, as you noted *pace* Creon ... things can always get worse ... moreover and also, en plus, encore and fourth ... we cannot always account for the interventions of the MOP ... we cannot *(coughs again)* ... hem, hem ... rely on interagency cooperation ...

two: *(looking across)* ... the MOP's not looking very well, is it? ...

one: *(locating glasses and peering over)* ... no, to be fair, 't isn't ... it is, truth be told, *not* ... but then again 'm not sure it ever did ... don't know how much luck you get in the looks department if you're stitched up from the discarded waste products ... the exuvia ... of larval incarnations ...

two: *(looking again and appraising)* ... sometimes I feel a bit sorry for the MOP, gildy ...

one: ... yes, I can see from whence you are coming, but let us not concern

ourselves overly too much with the MOP agency, we all have our crosses to
crush us, my fatterling Schmetterling ...

two: *(queasy)* ... gildy ... I think it's happening again ...

one: ... oh ... oh ...

two: ... here we go ... it is this deep blankness ...

one: ... the real thing s-t-r-a-n-g-e ...

*(well, old hypocrite lecteur, semblable and the rest ... by now – if you're still there at all, you
know the pack drill: the obligatory SSE followed by the optional FPTA ⟶)*

Part IV Mother

thread

What. I ask. Are we. To do. With our RAGE? Cx

fury

When they convene over your ashes| in a stylish,
mournful way| and talk their oily platitudes| and speak
their oily say - || When they dress up in respectful black|
and understated shoes| and tell their hearts are broken|
and tell you were their muse - || I will not be silent| I will
snarl with rage| I will roar with fury| and I will storm
their stage.|| And with my teeth or implement| or any
given thing| I'll make my peace with Justice| and I'll do
the f***ers in ... jx

Damn straight. Cx

Alternatively, if we're Achilles we take off down the
beach and sulk for ten years. Not an option, however, for
maternal entities ... jx

donkey

One day - some years ago now -

a woman (and a mother too)

still young though,

her hope not spent,

went out

to do that round

of earthbound stuff

(A mother must).

Time passed.

And she came back

Having acquired

> - no one knows
>   not how, nor why -

a donkey

on a string.

She called it Tuesday

(whose child is full of grace).

Her name was Judith.

This is a true story

(And those were surely magic beans).

(late for Bernard's birthday, May 2005)

things not to speak about   i

See how she goes with her needle and thread
sewing the baby's brains in its head
and snipping it now for an arm and a wrist
cutting out hands with a tear and a twist.

Over and under: again and again
inside to outside then knotting the ends;
neck bowed and rocking she twines as she frets
blood, flesh and bone into heartbeat and breath.

But work - and she does work - she never can know
every sinister night time swerve of her soul;
the baby is bonded to be what she dreads -
her unspeakable sin - wrought through every thread.

Turn around - leave them to shift as they may:
pray the hems hold fast when the fraught seams fray

refrain: *rip the sinews from my body*
tear my body from my mind
I have loved you over edges
that sever space from time.

things not to speak about   ii

say mouth is hole and pot to put it in

say mouth is shape and madness rimming it

say mouth is mind and darkness filling it

say mouth is mother and mother's tongue speaking it :

so hewn by hungers and betrayed by lust

she haunts each nightmare for what has been lost

till daylight dials in its steep toll of shame :

she should not have put so much in it again.

why must she throw herself over the edge

fling herself, rush herself off every ridge :

the fall is too deep, love, for feet to reach ground

they are all gone for ever - can never be found.

Oh help each human thing, women and men:

she put too much in - and it's empty again.

refrain : *tear the membranes of my body*
rip the brainstem from my mind
I love you past the limit-point
that structures space and time.

things not to speak about   iii

There is nothing left and all hope has gone.
They are too far out. Have fallen too far down.

The body is broken. The brainstem's snapped
She did what she could do. None of it worked.

- Is there no little thought will come to me now?
  These are my last knees. I can bear no more.

  Any help? From anywhere? Out here in the dark.
  I did all I could do. None of it worked.

- Make yourself - (make myself) - make yourself - find
  the tiniest etch of a thread in your mind :

  Take your last bit of breath - (with this my last breath) -
  breathe the love you have borne back into the thread.

Cross the great wide dark see old aching fingers sew
little wordbits into worlds : - and the baby into gold.

refrain: *stop the heartbeat in my body*
take this my furthest breath
I will love beyond the borderline
that severs life from death.

etched II

Repudiation of consequentiality

When the common is lost . . .

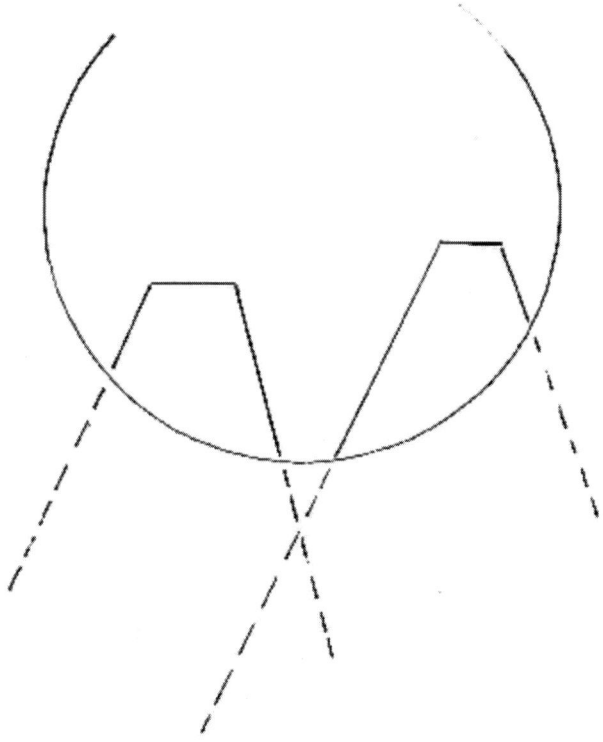

. . . can nothing else hold consequence?

wager

(or: I am not a betting man)

I went all in

with word and thing

and kept them yanked - together -

(though they would spin

and swerve

apart)

with scraps of thread

smeared glue, some string

a desperate stitch

a rusting pin:

an any kind of anything.

It was my Teufelspakt.

My greedy sin.

I could not know

I did not know

if any bit, or all of it,

at all

would hold.

The stake itself was soul.

- and there you are

- and here you are

compact and hidden glory

the matter of your fact

this (extra) ordinary story

of our fully paid-out bet.

Thank *you* for that.

(for jgb from jg)

go fly

go fly my son - and I
will wave and wave and wave
and tears will fall down my face
stretched wide with joy to see you go.

and my heart will break - and break again -
with loving and hoping more
than a body can bear. That we
you and me - have cut the string -

that bound us up in always
fear and failing. Go fly
my sweet imperfect son.
My - our - penance is done.

(for igb from jg)

stone and bind and tree

When he was savaged by his angel
in the desert - quite alone:
when he dreamt his sacred ladder -
Jacob's pillow was a stone.

When Isaac saved his father
from the glamour of his death:
unbinding mortal sacrifice -
he had song upon his breath.

When Eve stretched for the apple
and bit into her desire:
she brought forth human history -
from all that holy fire.

O happy for stone and bind and tree : -
to have borne the blazing of these three!

(for J, and I and E)

old, old women

we are old, we are old, we are old, nearly dead
we are women with no breasts or brains in our head
we are useless, we are toothless, we are stupid and unseen
we scavenge in the dirt where nothing is clean -

   -   but oh my fair, my sweetest fair
       what has happened to that long black hair
       and where is the light in those wide brown eyes
       and the red, red twist of those lips that kissed -

       oh my fair, my sweetest fair
       what has happened to that lovely there?

                  - gone, love, gone
                    for a stitch and a song

                    done, quite done
                    on a game not won

                    spent, yes, spent
                    and still more lent

                    paid, all paid
                    on a cloth that frayed

                    lost, love, lost
                    an impossible cost.

   -   but why, my fair, my sweetest one
       why is it gone for a stitch and a song
       why quite done on a game not won?
       and if it's done and gone and spent
       why more to be paid and lost and lent?

- it was the sin that did it in
and shame that wrecked the game

it was brave intent that lent and
spent
and things to be made for what was
paid

and it was love that lost and cost
the most.

we are old, we are old, we are old, clearly mad
we have passed all the places where there's pleasure to be had
we are formless, we are senseless, we are barren and obscene
we have nothing left of what we might have been.

(for my darling fair, incomparably Claire)

damn well tree

(i)

a mindless walk through winter air
till things emerge - there's nothing there

but - now - instants in front of me
the formal matter of this tree

(and causes great perplexity).

(ii)

So.

I come each day to stand and see
what is the thing about this tree ...
some knowledge that's resisting me
stumped here, in dumb stupidity

(though I inquire repeatedly).

I try poem words. Like dark and bare.
These torsion branches - stark: austere.
A syntax both obscure and clear
hierogamos of earth and air.

(and I could get that stuff to fly
but it would be untrue. An easy lie.)

So back again, I go, to see
what? Is the thing about this tree?

This damn well tree.
And damn well me.

(iii)

So. Here is tree

tree

And here is me

me

Thus we can say:

tree   me

And then.
Hooray!

I come to see
the space between

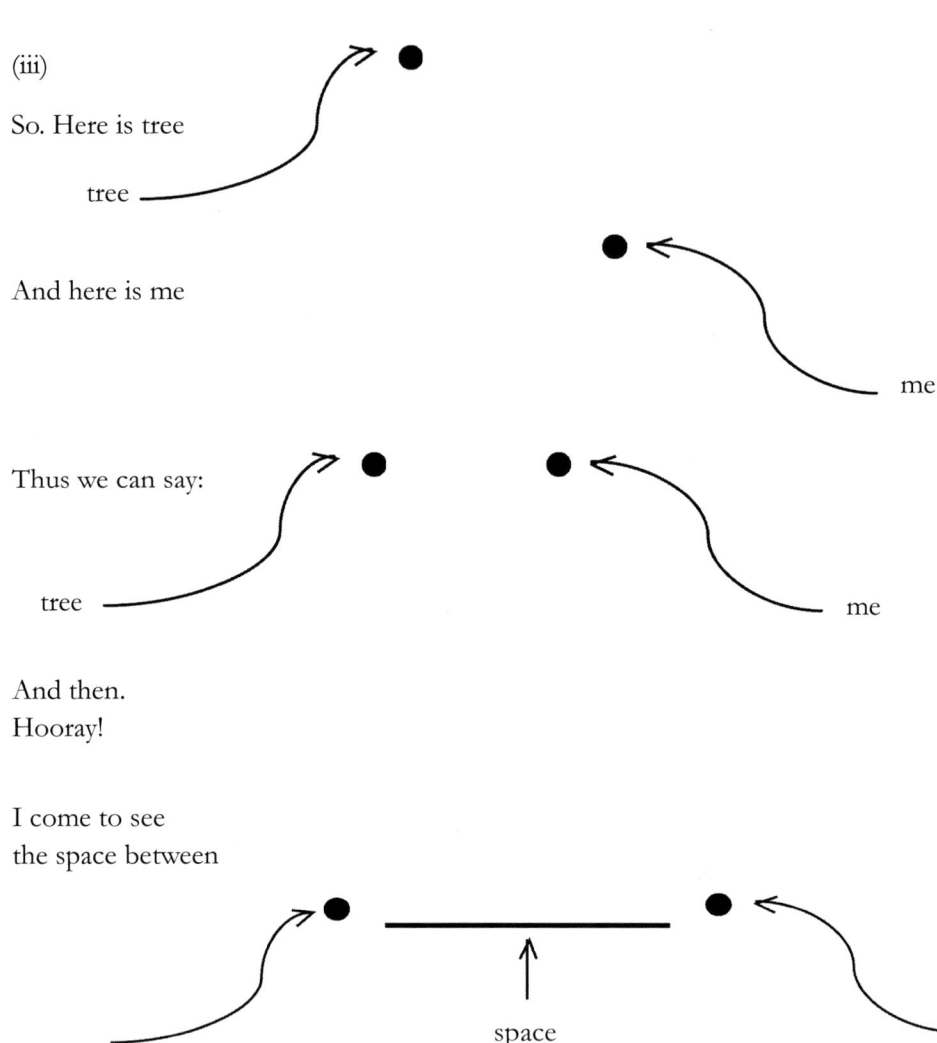

tree   space   m

that makes us: not one, not two,
but one, two, three -
and is, foundational of
reality

or, at least,
representational possibility.

(iv)

With that, I hope, enough's been said
and I can haul myself to bed.

But.

No.

      It seems these feet are bound
to trudge across this sodden land
and pitch again, before the tree,
as though there's something more to see.

So. On.
And on.

      With the daily stand
in wet and cold, flood-mudded ground.
The tree, obliquely, scanning me
for a logic that I cannot see.

Ah!

Feet have dredged a new idea:

They try standing far. And standing near.
And. Yes! There might be something here -

for in this problem of the tree
there's the matter of propinquity.

If I stop too far to stand and see

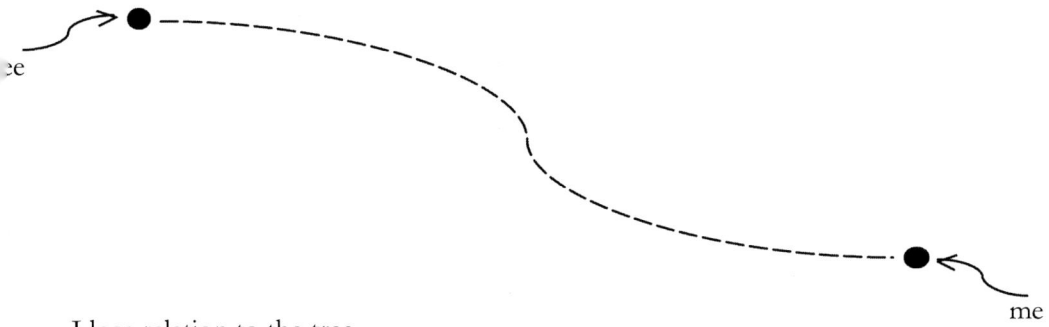

ee

me

I lose relation to the tree.

But, if, on the other hand,
I go in very close to stand -

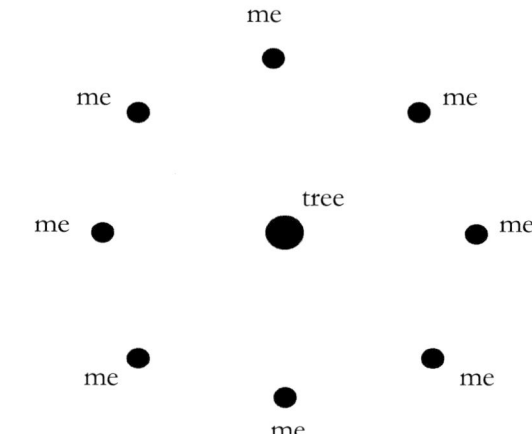

I find I'm occluded out by tree
and have very little sense of me.

Well.

Then I try a different test.
Trekking from north/east/south or west

Thusly it's made clear to me
there's a right relation with the tree
that's roughly equidistantly.

So its not to do with north/north west
That marks a certain standpoint best
but more to do with near or far
that makes tree-relations -
- what they are.

(v)

And if upon this foot-stod ground
I plot the points and tramp all round

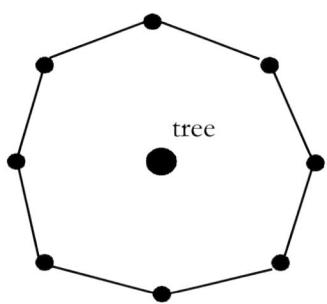

I've traced a ring, a boundary -
which simply is: - I come to see,
the *in/out* premise - of identity.

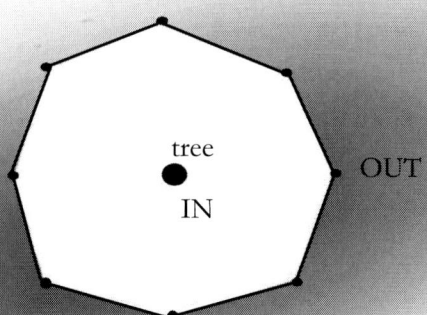

Structure both of prison -
- and of sanctuary.

(vi)

And after that - I'm made aware -
there's the *down* in earth, the *up* in air
necessary substantiality
of (multi) dimensionality

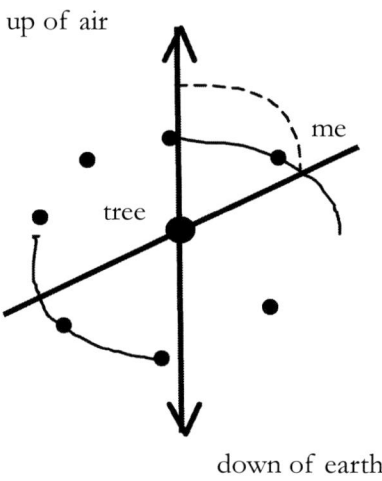

up of air

me

tree

down of earth

And from tree and ring and earth and air
comes forth this pro-ject of a sphere.

So me and tree stuck planted here
in mud-logged feet and freezing air
there's still the grinding need to ask
why? keep on with such a task?

(vii)

But damn well feet and their drudging stand
Rooted in storm-wasted ground.

Where.

On considering its place
(in the wider umwelt of time-space)
I see the membrane of my pro-ject sphere
emerges only from its outer layer.

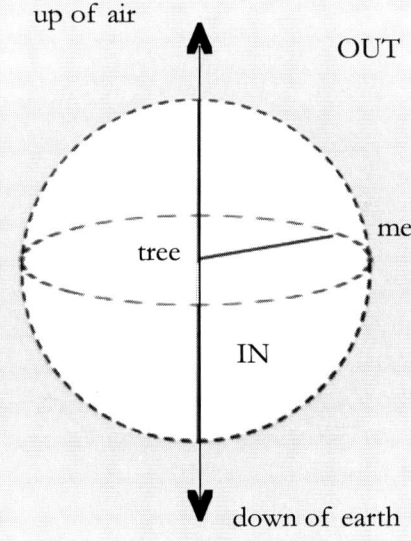

So here's a stretching thing to think:
within is made from *outside* in.

(viii)

And then - throughbreaking - shouts a cheer
that alarms dog-walkers walking near

the thing is labouring to come clear - -
- - - as I induce the *evert* of my sphere.

For.

If it were a living, breathing thing : -
it would breathe in *out* and breathe out *in*.

And the baby's in, the baby's out
The baby's twisted all about.

And if the mother's outside, on her skin
The true fact is : - she's also in.

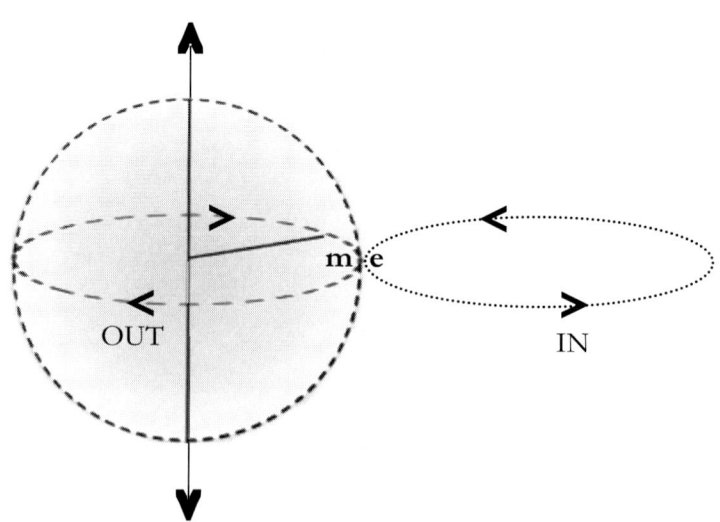

(ix)

And then.
Again!
I leap - -
- - in mud-splashing glee

For in this evert-sphere I see : -
possible
impossibility.

This sphere-evert created here
- invisible in earth and air -
something that you cannot *see*
that, nonetheless, can be made *to be*.

So *what* is the knowledge in this damn well tree?
Answer: the matter of
(maternal)
subjectivity.

Ha!

(x)

Thus in this tale of tree and me
(that's torn the edges of my sanity)
ancient logic of each mythic story -
worlds apart from power and glory.

Mother ∞ child - extorted - all about
in the agon to get who's inside, *out*
Without committing the primal sin
of butchering : -
who en/forms the *in*.

(xi)

Jesus.

But it **is** cold.
And I **am** old.
This tree chronicle.
Has now been told.

The end.

speech

Fifth ((sshhhhhh and final)) INSTAR

one: *(burping)* ... gezplupzt ... do excuse me, my rampling rosy ... to be quite honest, and sincere, I'm not sure how much more of this eating I can eat ....

two: *(reclining and lethargic)* ... no, me neither gildy ... I feel ... I feel ... I feel a little of what might be called ... monstrous ...

one: *(squinting down at the other, as reading glasses have snapped under the force of expansion)* ... not a bad term for it ... as Kant did usefully observe, *"an object is monstrous where by its size it defeats the end that informs its concept"* ... *(surveying its own not inconsiderable amplitude)* ... you would have thought we met the membership criteria ... *(suddenly swoony)* ... *whooooah* said Snowy ... it is as though there may be some kind of exploding event on the horizon ... imminently and looming ...

two: *(shaking head as vigorously as engorged larval form permits)* ... I do not at all like the sound of that, no sire, no siree, oh no, oh dear, uh-oh ... I do *not* like the sound of that, not *one* bit at all ...

one: ... no, can't say I'm keen ... moi non plus ... going around blowing up all over the place ... exploding like a bomb abroad ... not exactly *comme il faut* ...

two: ... jeepers gee whizz and creepers ... what ... is ... happening ... to my skin ... this isn't like the other times actually in actual matter of fact ...

one: *(also rattled)* ... I think ... if things are unfolding according to the logic of our allegory ... that we may be pupating ... ne t'inquiètes pas, ma cochonette rose, it will ... or may ... *jings!* ... just about ... all be for the best ... *(gasping)* ... in the best of all possible worlds ...

two: *(terrified)* ... h-e-l-p ... Vater, siehst du denn nicht ...

one and two togther: ... daß wir ver-br-e-nn-en ...

*(from the voidy echo sounding its sibilant **sssss** on eerie contact with the page, it is probable this address is redundant and, indeed, like A.E. Houseman's* cuckoo, *that shouts all day at nothing, is merely making an unpleasant noise in a vacuum. Oh well. Nevermind. It is surely evident that it's petty pace is almost crept ... might be just as well to strutt and frett on to the end ...)*

Part V **Paths**

thread

Up periscope ... ! ... Cx

the woman and the apple tree in spring

deep in the dense compacted branch
there is the whisper of the bud -

        - will she come?
        - I cannot tell
            she comes from heaven and from hell -

high in the spare impassive air
suspends a space that may suspire -

        - is she here?
        - I cannot say
            she may be near or far away -

bold now the sweet transgressive buds
tease the discretion of their branch -

        - does she speak?
        - I am not sure
            she uses words not heard before -

wide in the loud candescent air
the shock of blossom in blazing choir -

        - is she real?
        - I do not know
            she leaves a trail of burning snow -

        fall away and fade : fall away and grieve -
        we will always be traduced by love.

(late, yet again, for Bernard's birthday)

dear Bernard,

Here is a version of the path poem I have been working on – it may be useful (or indeed not) in your thinking on the sigilum. This digital version has only just been constructed – until now have been fiddling endlessly about with piles of cut out letters on the rug.

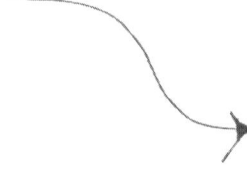

Dear Judith,

That's lovely – and forceful. It's a space that holds my line within it. It's an assertion, a question [does it really have an exclamation in it?].
The poem leads on, also – to the structure of a space, to what comes from an investigation of paths.

dear Bernard,

Yes!? The path through the woods poem is both an assertion and the ironic questioning of the structure of assertion, which, as you pointed out, is one of the ways of inveigling a tiny path of life through the implacable granite vale of deathness that is obsessional neurosis.

With regard to your sigil – I think the poem works to make formal how femininity must come on terms with the necessity (Ananke) of limits; of the limits of language and in language in order that she might en/corporate more of the spaces beyond (jenseits). For without this enacted tethering, she would just fall from the edges, fall without end, into the empty nothingness, which is not the nothing of negation.

Dear Judith,

I have had flu. These phrases – the *Ananke* of limits, and *enacted tethering* – helped me to move out of it.

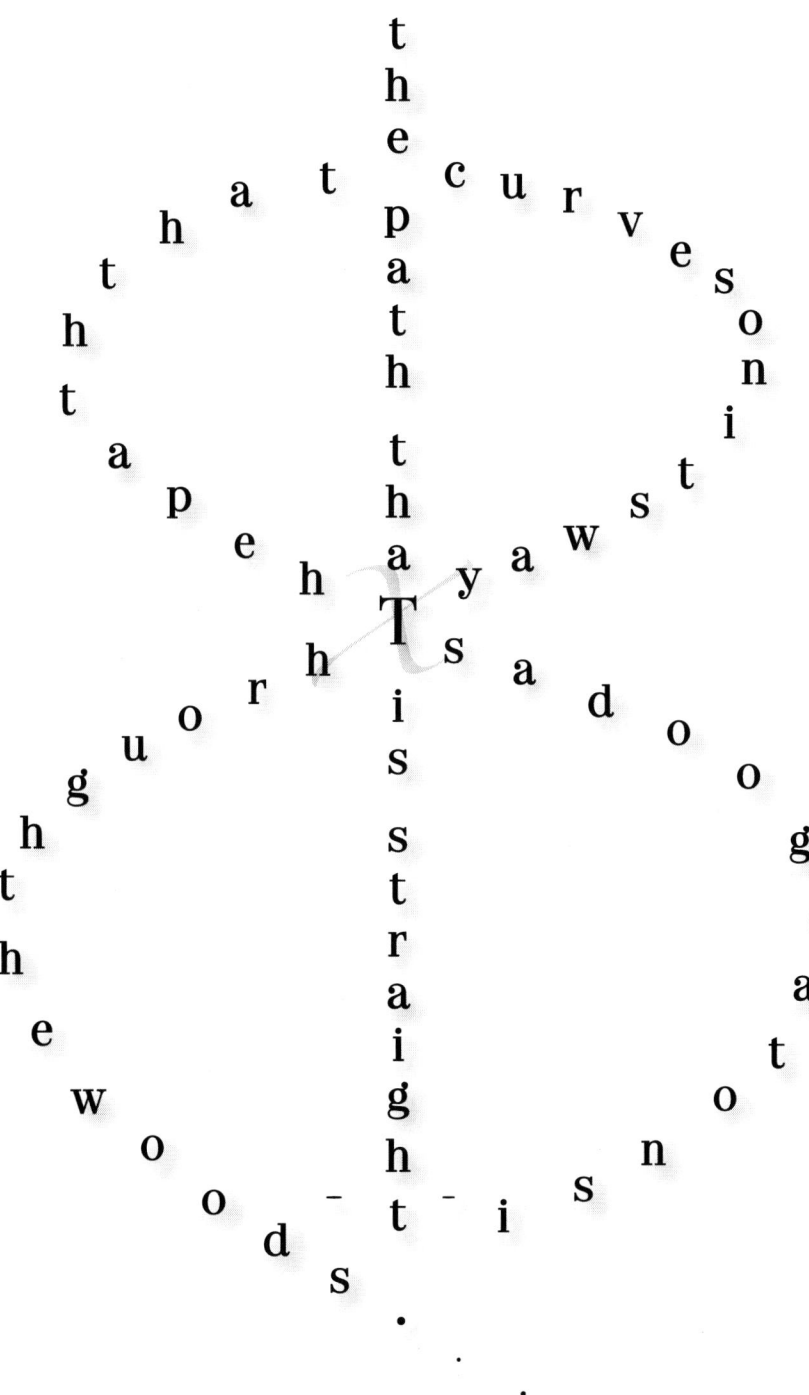

father of the grey seas

beyond the stormy Hebrides

on the pitch-most rock before the seas

are all-entirely gulfed by seas

- and seas by skies, or counterwise -

an old and ancient sea-shag stands

cragged by blast of storm and time

solitary stroke of black-etched line

amid the vast and formless brine:

father of the grey seas

hope

a silver thread

a golden bell

and a blackbird

in the apple tree.

(little haiku of hope for egb from jg)

two women, naked *contd*

(continued from here . . .)

two women, naked
one is submerged
and drowning
deep
in a tank of water
the other hangs over the edge
necessarily having tethered her foot or ankle
uneasily
to a wooden post on the outside
she is suspended also
deep
in the tank

and,
in what appears to be a kiss,
delivers a mouthful of air
in her breath
to the
drowning
other

two women, naked
with thick, beautiful jewel coloured
ribbons
cats-cradled between them
from their outstretched hands
forming the most deft and delicate
intrication
gleaming warp and weft
living net of ribbons

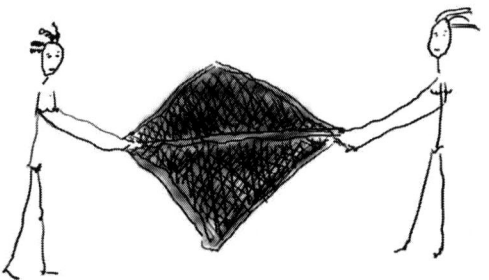

two women, naked
dancing a dithyramb

with the most
abundant
peony roses

woven in
woven in

etched III

Art shows while it hides: it traces the lineaments of the Real

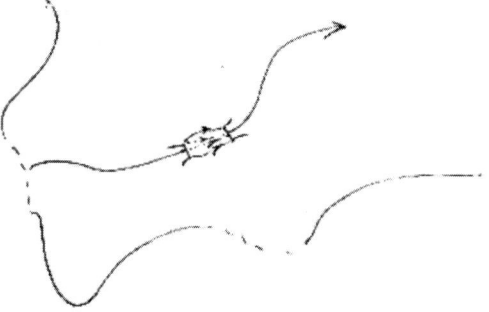

Art presents the real – as art of enacted tethering

bb

bird

i.

... there, on the branch: a bird

- just gone -

and left behind

- air -

wrung with song

ii.

how strange

iii.

to think the absence of a vital presence

overlaid   in space   by its own negation

is, in fact, the matter of creation

iv.

oh blazing moment :

living word

- the sound of Homer -

(being heard).

(jg for bb, january 2011)

fort da

for many years - more than those lived -
(more now by far) - I have thought on her -
her who was called my mother.
And in the hollow thrum of the pulse
I have nearly always drowned.

Not that this is not love. It is not never love.
That is not it. No, not that at all.
In this case, take love as an iron given,
bond of interminable and deadly play
the totalised presence of utter absence
- an unfree state.

No. What it is. After all these years
(of asking what) - it is that I want -
her not just here with me, for always here,
(for we grow old and ill and people die). No.
I want her out there,
in diadem - bejewelled nocturnal array
Burnished.
A shining star.

In which situation, I can
- be somewhat apart -
and can wipe the tears with the end of my sleeve
and nudge my neighbour (seated also)
and say : -

"See her,
her over there
 - she who's not me -
that's my mother.

Isn't it a fine thing."

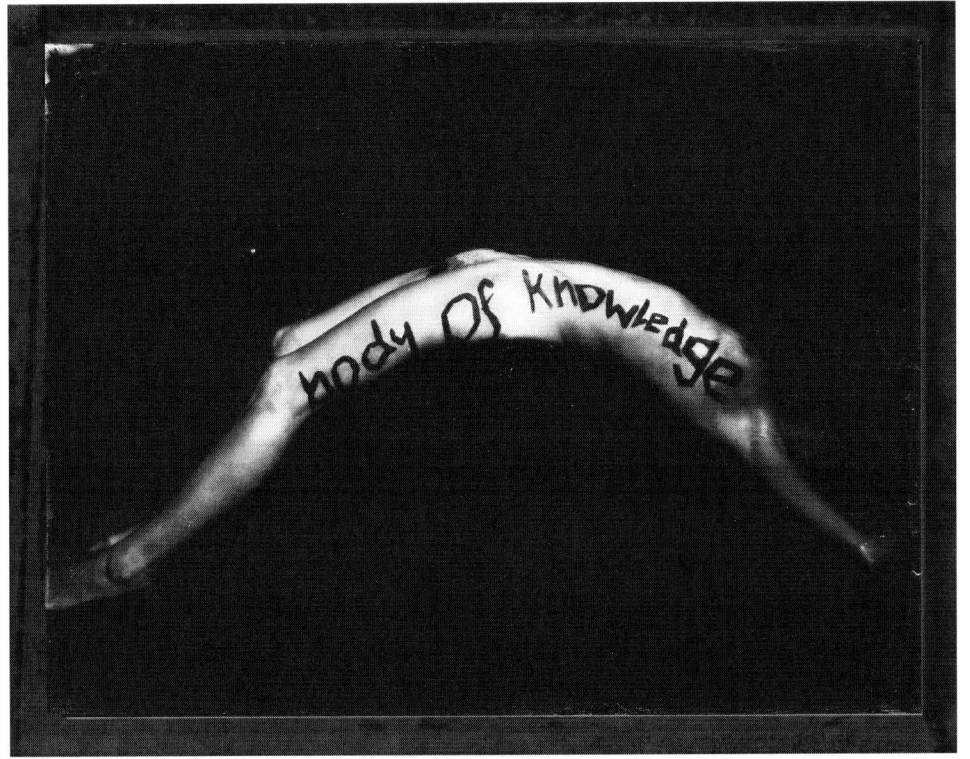

nunc dimittis . . .

germ _ _ gilda
    gilda
    rosy-pants_and
    ars...

"... fools! . . . for we also

in the end . . .

had our hour" . . .

is our beginning . . .

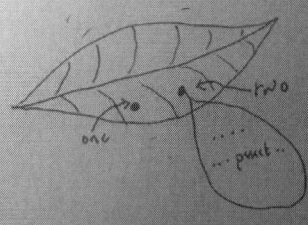

~~done~~ (?) - donk (!)

wo Es war ... soll eine Eselin werden

Acknowledgements ...

To Alexandra Thornton, who stepped over every line with me, and again and again over, in the design and layout of this work.

To Mr McBratney, Sir, Tom for all those Friday afternoons translating every **** word of Antigone and for checking the Greek (by which subtile acknowledgement, I shuffle onto you the buck ...)

To Jacob Gracie-Burrow for the ongoing dialectic and specifically for the formula that you cannot be a mother and be a writer, arrived at when discussing Frankenstein before his finals at Oxford.

To Simon Rosenberg for invaluable last minute technical rescue.

To Adam Searle, formerly at the Royal Marsden, and his team, for all their care over all these so many years.

To Ros Eeles and her team at the Royal Marsden, for everything, for each and every one of us.

To Prof Collins at the Royal Brompton, for mending me when I was broken.

To Simon Davies at the Royal Brompton, for passing me onto Prof Collins when we were at a loss.

To Doctors Morgenstein, Munro and Feher, and all at Beta Cell, Chelsea and Westminster Hospital for their ongoing care.

To the Hormone and Gynaecology teams at the Chelsea and Westminster, particularly Claire Bellone, for finding ways both surgical and non-surgical, that enabled me to keep on keeping on.

To Laura Wade at Chiswick Dental Practice for gentle perseverance in dealing with the hell of DKA-ravaged teeth.

To Jane Bridges at the Chelsea and Westminster who kept me in play when I haemorrhaged on her table, back in the day.

To the staff of A & E at Ealing Hospital for the consistent attentive care over many years and visits.

To all at Corfton Road Surgery, Ealing for everything they have done – and hopefully will continue to do – to help over many years.

To Temple Pharmacy, Pitshanger Lane for their kind efficiency, discretion and support.

To Louise Picton Pegg, for looking after me, while I thought mad thoughts on wild walks, up and down the north Norfolk coast.

To Amy Moore for curly, and Sue King for crazy, hair.

And to Karnac Books for giving me this book.

"I've traced a ring, a boundary –
which simply is: - I come to see
the in/out premise – of identity.

Structure both of prison
– and of sanctuary."